Artistic Wildlife Projects
for the Scroll Saw

by Marilyn Carmin

Fox
Chapel Publishing Co. Inc.

1970 Broad Street • East Petersburg, PA 17520 • www.foxchapelpublishing.com

Publisher	Alan Giagnocavo
Book Editor	Ayleen Stellhorn
Project Editor	Gretchen Bacon
Cover Design	Jon Deck
Desktop Specialist	Alan Davis

ISBN 1–56523–224–0
Library of Congress Control Number: 2003116104

To order your copy of this book,
please send check or money order
for the cover price plus $3.50 shipping to:
Fox Books
1970 Broad St.
East Petersburg, PA 17520
1-800-457-9112

Or visit us on the web at **www.foxchapelpublishing.com**

Printed in China

10 9 8 7 6 5 4 3 2 1

Because scrolling wood inherently includes the risk of injury and damage, this book cannot guarantee that creating the projects in this book is safe for everyone. For this reason, this book is sold without warranties or guarantees of any kind, expressed or implied, and the publisher and author disclaim any liability for any injuries, losses or damages caused in any way by the content of this book or the reader's use of the tools needed to complete the projects presented here. The publisher and the author urge all scrollers to thoroughly review each project and to understand the use of all tools involved before beginning any project.

Acknowledgments

Thank you, Garth, for your love, patience, encouragement, humor and support. I love you!

ABOUT THE AUTHOR

Born and raised in southern California, Marilyn became interested in both art and nature at an early age. Her first blue ribbon was awarded for a kindergarten finger painting. As her skills developed, she found that the foundation for most of her art is wildlife.

Over the years, Marilyn has worked with many different mediums but continually finds herself drawn to wood. The scroll saw has given Marilyn the perfect opportunity to combine her art with wood.

Marilyn and her husband, Garth, currently reside in the Pacific Northwest—an area full of inspiration.

TABLE OF CONTENTS

Introduction

The purpose of this book is to encourage you to think outside the box, to push you to try something different, to help you realize your artistic capabilities, and to edge you past any self-imposed limits.

Remember that the patterns in this book are meant to be manipulated. Don't be afraid to cut them or use them in other ways. Have fun experimenting. Laugh when things don't work quite as planned and savor the pride you feel when they do!

In order to cut the patterns in this book, you'll need a solid knowledge of scroll saw basics. My focus is not on teaching you *how* to scroll, but on teaching you how to scroll *creatively*. To that end, I have included an entire section of wildlife patterns with instructions and tips on altering them. I've also included hints on choosing wood and accessories and on displaying your projects.

I hope the information compiled will help you expand and grow.

— Marilyn Carmin

Original Pattern 1

Original Pattern 2

New Pattern

Figure 1. By combining the focal point of Original Pattern 1 and the background of Original Pattern 2, we create a more dynamic new pattern.

PART ONE

Making a Scroll Saw Project Your Own

Now that you've mastered some of the basics of scrolling, you may be looking for ways to improve or expand your capabilities. Perhaps you've discovered a talent or preference for intarsia. Maybe you love fretwork. Whatever your particular talent or direction for growth, this chapter is intended to give you methods, from simple to complex, to hone your skills and to stretch your artistic limits. We will specifically focus on changing your patterns and presenting your work to fit your preferences.

CHANGING THE PATTERN

To begin changing your patterns, select your pattern of choice and categorize its parts. You'll especially want to look for the focal point and the background of the pattern. The focal point is the part of the pattern that demands the most attention. Very often it is physically in the center of the pattern. Generally, the background constitutes any part of the pattern that is not the focal point. Take a look at Original Pattern 1 in Figure 1. In this example the owl is our focal point, the most interesting part of the pattern. The branches and the oval shape make up the background, as they are less interesting and help to focus the viewer's attention on the owl. Now that we've identified the pattern parts, we're ready to make some changes.

The first way to change a pattern is to work with the focal point. Highlight that focal point, photocopy the pattern, and discard the undesired background. Look through other patterns for a possible complementary background. Photocopy the complementary background, enlarging or shrinking it as needed. Then place the focal point over the background and move the parts around to find the best fit. Try different pattern combinations. **(See Figure 1.)**

For this type of alteration, a light box is helpful. Using a light box eliminates the time spent cutting, fitting and pasting only to find the finished pattern doesn't have the look you envisioned. Being able to view several layers of pattern at once allows you to shift layers around and gain different perspectives before you cut and paste. If you do not own a light box, a piece of glass set across a separated dining room table with a lamp underneath works fine. Also, many copy stores have light boxes available for customer use.

When you are incorporating patterns, some adjustments will be necessary to give the new design a sense of cohesion. First, pay attention to connecting the two so the pattern does not end up in pieces when cut. Second, when attaching the two patterns, avoid a cookie-cutter look. **(See Figure 2.)** Cookie cutters leave a very symmetrical, identical and evenly spaced look. The goal is to avoid all three of these. The pattern elements should flow together as though they were always part of the same design. Varying the spacing and lines of the connections achieves a more spontaneous look. It also helps to have an odd number of connections—one, three, five or seven. This also contributes to a spontaneous and natural look. Lastly, if you have your own ideas, don't be afraid to try them. This makes the pattern even more your own.

Using the background is the second way to change a pattern. This method is a reverse of the first method. Select a background that you find appealing and choose a

Highlighting the Focal Point

1. Choose a focal point.
2. Remove all undesired elements from around the focal point.
3. Choose a complementary background from a second pattern.
4. Integrate the two to make a new pattern.

focal point to complement it. Using a copier, size to fit, connect the patterns and, voilà, a new design. A good example of an interesting

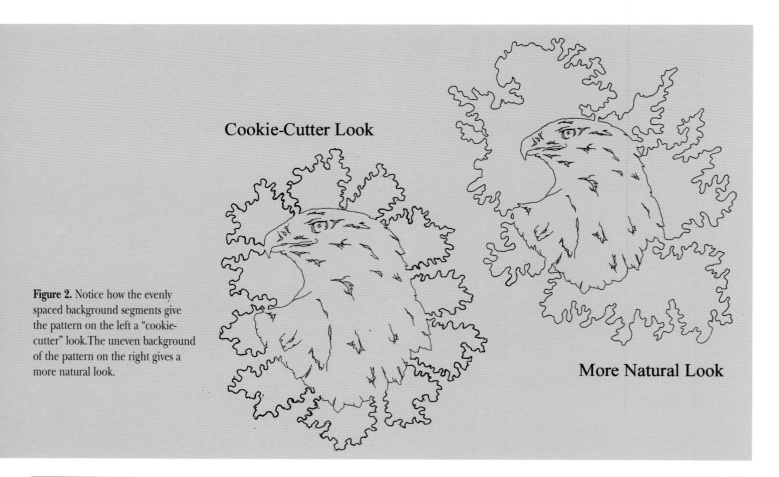

Cookie-Cutter Look

More Natural Look

Figure 2. Notice how the evenly spaced background segments give the pattern on the left a "cookie-cutter" look. The uneven background of the pattern on the right gives a more natural look.

Using an Interesting Background

1. Choose a background.
2. Remove the undesired elements and/or focal point.
3. Choose a complementary focal point from a second pattern.
4. Integrate the two to make a new pattern.

Adding Enhancements

1. Select a main pattern and an enhancement pattern.
2. Add the enhancement pattern to the main pattern as desired.

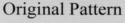

Figure 3. By simply removing one eagle, we create a new pattern.

Original Pattern   New Pattern

background is the "Feather" pattern. (See page 58.)

Third, try using a small portion of a pattern that you find appealing. Maybe the original pattern features two eagles. Remove one eagle, and the other becomes your new pattern. **(See Figure 3.)**

Fourth, use these same steps to add to an existing design. Enhancing a mammal design, like a wolf or a bear, with footprints is a great addition to a pattern. Often the original design is a good, solid pattern; however, the addition of footprints "walking" across the surface, inserted into a corner, or outlining the focal point may furnish the finishing touch that places your work above another. **(See Figure 4.)**

Finally, a very easy change is to simply reverse a design. That is, if the design is facing left, turn it so

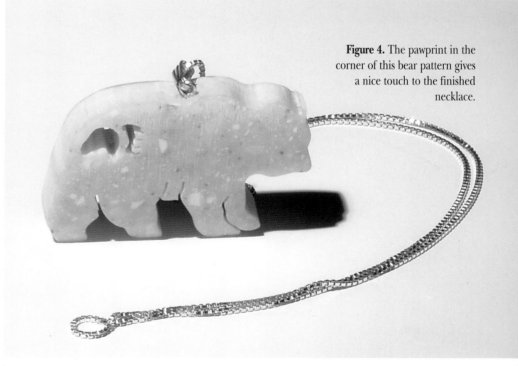

Figure 4. The pawprint in the corner of this bear pattern gives a nice touch to the finished necklace.

Figure 5. Flipping a design from left to right is an easy way to change a pattern.

that it is facing right. Very often this reversal of a design is exactly what is needed. **(See Figure 5.)**

USING DIFFERENT TECHNIQUES

Changing a pattern from one technique to another—fretwork becomes overlay, relief becomes inlay, and inlay becomes intarsia— takes some trial and error, but it is well worth the effort. Though a pattern may have been drawn with a

certain technique in mind, a few simple changes shift the pattern to a new technique.

When you are changing patterns from one technique to another, there are certain cutting lines that will be eliminated or changed; however, it's important that the changes do not affect the integrity of the design. To keep the physical strength of a design, certain lines need to connect. It will take some experience to recognize these elements, but your attempts will bring experience and, eventually, success. Play with different techniques. Sometimes changes don't work; sometimes additional changes are necessary, but with each of these "experiments" comes knowledge which results in future sucesses.

Converting to Overlay

1. Determine the different layers by deciding which elements are closest to and farthest from the viewer. The closest elements become the foreground, the farthest elements become the background, and the in-between elements become the middle ground.
2. Choose your woods with the desired look in mind.
3. Complete each piece; then glue the layers together.

OVERLAY

Instead of cutting a design as a single layer, try an overlay. Using the overlay technique adds new dimension to a design. Instead of the one-dimensioned project your pattern was destined to be, you now have a blueprint for added depth and interest. Divide the pattern into layers: a foreground, a background and possibly a middle ground. **(See Figure 6.)** Cut and

Original Pattern

New Forground Pattern

New Background Pattern

Figure 6. To create an overlay, break the pattern sections apart. Here the foreground and the background of the original pattern become the overlay patterns.

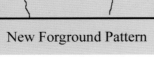

1. Decide which direction the design faces.
2. Turn it the opposite direction.

1. Choose which elements of the pattern will be recessed, normal or pushed out.
2. Tilt the saw table the desired number of degrees.
3. Cut the layers; then push out or recess the desired parts.
4. Glue as necessary.

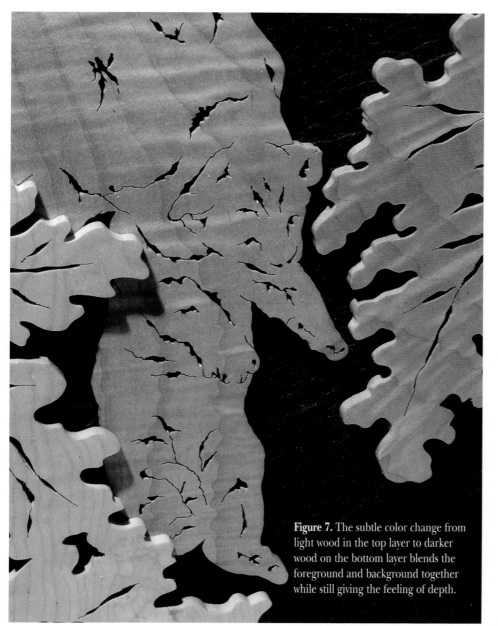

Figure 7. The subtle color change from light wood in the top layer to darker wood on the bottom layer blends the foreground and background together while still giving the feeling of depth.

stack the layers. If you want to create more depth, insert wooden spacers between each piece.

Contrasting wood can be effective in combination with overlay. Major contrast, both in color and intensity, makes a strong statement. The overlay is more prominent and important. Less contrast in woods achieves a soft blending of design with a gentle flow between the background and the overlay. **(See Figure 7.)** Although overlays can be cut in thick wood, ½ inch or ¼ inch seems to work best. Thick overlays have a tendency to give the completed artwork a "chunky," heavy or out-of-balance appearance. Remember, if the background is too busy, the focal point is lost.

RELIEF

The relief technique allows you to add a "carved" look to a design while still using your scroll saw. This is an excellent technique to use when adding footprints to wildlife patterns. By tilting the saw table two

Converting to Intarsia

1. Choose the planes and divisions for each element of the pattern. The elements closest to the viewer become the foreground, the farthest elements become the background, and the in-between elements become the middle ground.
2. Choose your woods with the desired look in mind.
3. Cut and sand each piece to the desired height.
4. Glue to a backing board.

to three degrees to the right and cutting counterclockwise, the footprints will be recessed. This gives the impression that the animal walked across the wood. (**See Figure 8.**) This technique also works well to bring a total design into relief. A pattern that is normally cut away from the surrounding wood is cut from the wood but not removed. Instead, it is pushed into relief, and the surrounding wood becomes the background.

INTARSIA

Intarsia is a scroll saw technique that creates a "picture" out of wood by sanding different-colored woods to varying heights and contours. Pattern changes for intarsia take some definite thought, as decisions must be made on where to divide the pattern. Some of these divisions are more obvious than others. The place to start with a flower might be with an individual petal. The start-

Figure 8. This recessed pawprint gives the impression that the bear "walked" across the wood.

Converting to Inlay

1. Simplify the pattern by removing all unnecessary definition and veining lines.
2. Eliminate inside cuts or turn any inside cuts into inlaid sections.
3. Choose your woods with the desired look in mind.
4. Cut and finish each piece.
5. Glue together as necessary.

Converting to Fretwork

1. Study your pattern and decide where inside cuts, or frets, would best enhance the design.
2. Check that your inside cuts will not compromise the cohesion or structural integrity of the design.
3. Cut and finish as desired.

ing place with mammals or birds may possibly be along the lines of the bone structure. Pay close attention to the eyes because if the eyes are not correct, the whole pattern will look strange.

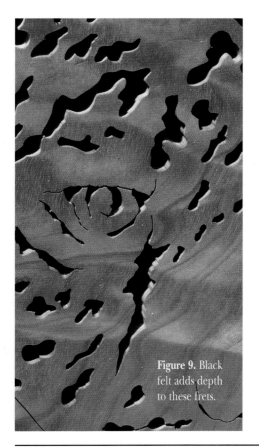

Figure 9. Black felt adds depth to these frets.

INLAY

Creating an inlaid piece involves stack cutting two or more pieces of different-colored wood; then combining these pieces to create a multi-colored finished project. Inlay is somewhat similar to relief, except the inlaid pieces remain flush with the rest of the project. Simplification is necessary for inlays. Veining and definition lines are removed. If not eliminated, inside cuts are often enlarged or combined and turned into inlaid areas. Silhouettes are the easiest patterns to change to inlays.

FRETWORK

With the addition of inside cuts, you are on your way to having a fretwork pattern. Added inside cuts must enhance the definition and shaping of the overall design without losing the focal point. It is also important that the physical strength of the design not be compromised.

CHANGING THE BACKDROP

Aside from the focal point of a piece, the backdrop sets the tone for a project. The elements of a backdrop—the color, the texture and the material used—can all affect how the onlooker feels when viewing the work. Textured leather, felt and colored paper are all examples of backdrop choices.

When choosing the backdrop for your project, first consider where the piece will be displayed. A blue backdrop may not be the best choice if the finished artwork is to be hung on a red wall. Whenever possible, take the project with you when choosing the backdrop; this will give you an opportunity to compare materials. A subtle difference in the backdrop can be the determining factor between a good piece and a great one.

Simply changing the backdrop color of a project can create a very different impression. A dark backdrop, for example, can add depth and will darken the cut-out and shadowed areas. **(See Figure 9.)** Try experimenting with colors other than the typical black or brown: Deep blues, greens and reds still add the shadows and depth but

Figure 10. The white backdrop offsets the dark wood.

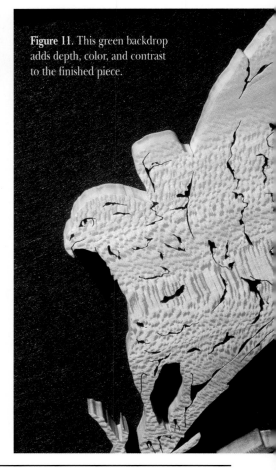

Figure 11. This green backdrop adds depth, color, and contrast to the finished piece.

project a different look. If you are using dark wood, a light backdrop may be the best choice. Reds and yellows add warmth whereas blues and greens create coolness. Bright colors add intensity to a design and can suggest a style or look. Bright purple or gold adds richness; red can project an oriental flair. **(See Figures 10 and 11.)**

Introduce different textures. The richness of velvet, the smoothness of acrylic plastic, or the ruggedness of burlap—all used in the correct applications—will greatly enhance a design. **(See Figures 12 and 13.)**

Many other materials can be used for backdrops, each with its own unique qualities. Leather often complements slab or burl wood. **(See Figure 14.)** Unfinished and weathered wood, photographs, plastic, mirrors, window screen, handmade paper, fabric, vinyl and metal are only a few of the materials to try. Stained glass has the unique ability to capture light within a design. Glass also makes it possible to backlight a project or to hang it in a window. The American flag behind a bald eagle makes a powerful statement.

Mix and match. You never know how your project might turn out. A combination might not work the first time, but you will have learned

valuable information for making your next project using similar elements. Try a bronze mirror behind an oriental fretwork or a photograph of a sunset behind a wildlife silhouette. Rich blue velvet with tiny silver stars may be the perfect backdrop to a Christmas project. Don't be afraid to try. Your experiments will bring new ideas, and new ideas bring unique and beautiful art.

Figure 13. Green felt and a wooden frame create a clean, polished finish.

CHOOSING YOUR WOOD

Choice of wood can dramatically affect a design. The type, color, thickness and grain are all considerations when choosing wood. Like the backdrop, wood choice helps to set the tone for the artwork. Rough, weathered wood can contribute ruggedness, cragginess and possibly even harshness to a project. Polished, refined elegance is more likely realized with a smooth, sanded, cleanly finished wood.

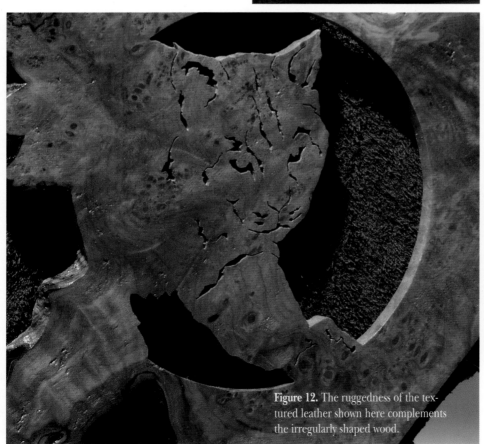

Figure 12. The ruggedness of the textured leather shown here complements the irregularly shaped wood.

Figure 14. Mildly textured leather works well for this cougar cut in natural wood. The backdrop neither draws too much attention from the other parts of the project nor is overwhelmed by the natural wood.

Figure 15. The reddish brown wood color suggests the coat of a grizzly bear.

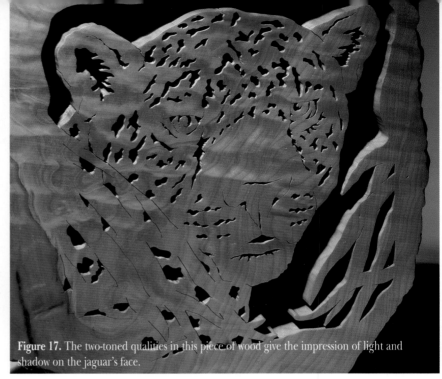

Figure 17. The two-toned qualities in this piece of wood give the impression of light and shadow on the jaguar's face.

Function and display also affect wood choice. A functional piece will hold up better in hard, rather than soft, wood. A piece displayed outside is best cut from wood that is resistant to the elements.

WOOD COLOR

Both the color and the tint of wood affect the finished piece. A dark wood adds heaviness; a light wood adds airiness. Techniques, too, can determine wood choice. Because dark wood can obliterate some fine detail, fretwork might be better set in light wood.

Variations in the color and the grain of some exotic woods will "tell" a person how to use it. Choosing chestnut's golden tan for a cougar or redwood for a fox are examples of realistic use of wood color. (See Figure 15.) Tiger myrtle (from Australia) looks like the coat of a cheetah; certain types of sycamore give the impression of a giraffe. One glance will tell you why zebrawood is so named.

WOOD GRAIN

As with color, the technique you choose and the fineness of the design affect grain choice. A dark-colored, heavy-grained piece of wood is perfect for a strong, bold design, but not for a delicate one.

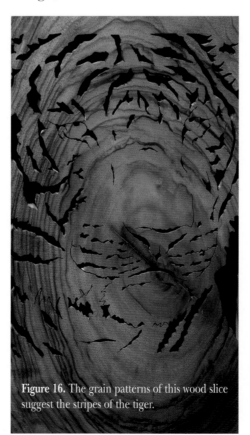

Figure 16. The grain patterns of this wood slice suggest the stripes of the tiger.

Grain especially adds the impression of texture, such as feathers on birds, mountains in the background or ripples in water. (See Figure 16.) Even the placement of knots can enhance a project.

When you find grain variations, use them to your advantage. A two-toned grain makes it possible to have your focal point one color with the supporting detail in another. (See Figure 17.) A log slab or slice often has the interior heartwood surrounded by a different color of sapwood. With careful layout, this is the perfect opportunity for a natural frame.

WOOD THICKNESS

The thickness of wood can make a difference in the overall appearance of a project. Although wood thickness is often decided by the pattern, by the pattern designer or even by convenience, playing with different thicknesses can be enlightening. A thinner piece of wood can add a light, delicate airiness, whereas a thicker wood may make a bold, strong statement.

Figure 18. Thin, light-colored wood makes this feather seem light and airy—almost as though it could float.

(See Figures 18 and 19.) Thick wood projects depth; thin wood projects delicateness. Some woods, like log cabin siding or moldings, vary in thickness. This gives each piece a unique and individual possibility. When choosing your wood thickness, be careful that the wood you choose isn't extreme in either direction. Wood that is too thin can create weaknesses in your project; wood that is too thick can overwhelm it.

One wood type is not better than another. Color, grain and thickness all enhance a project in different ways. The final wood choice is completely up to you.

IRREGULAR WOODS

Using burl wood, slab wood, oval limb slices or any irregular and natural-edged wood is another option for your projects. The uniqueness of these woods especially enhances the natural and rugged look of a wildlife design. Because the grain and the color of this type of wood can be extremely unusual, it is important that the wood and

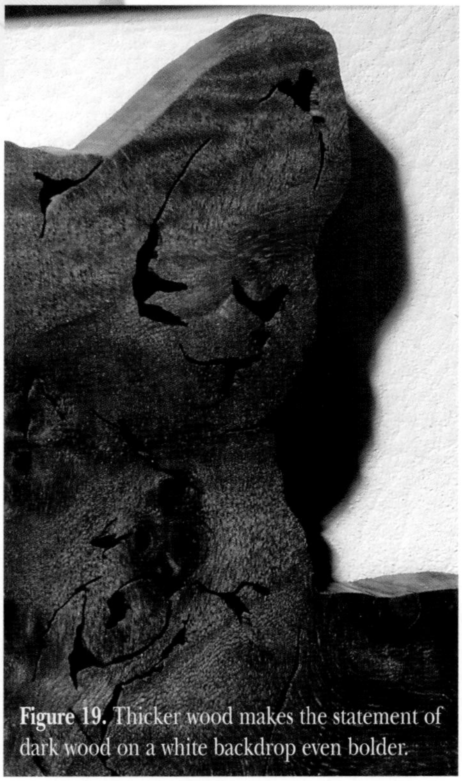

Figure 19. Thicker wood makes the statement of dark wood on a white backdrop even bolder.

the design complement each other. Many times the shape of the wood or the look of the grain will "suggest" a design. **(See Figure 16.)** Follow your instincts. It probably is best not to place a tractor design on a wood slab that reminds you of dolphins.

Irregular woods often allow you to experiment with design placement. Many times, designs are placed dead center because "that's

the way it's done"; however, some pieces might be better served with an atypical placement. Try mounting the pattern off-center, at one end, across the top or bottom, or along an edge.

The actual shape of the wood can have the capacity to determine placement. An irregular shape may give the appearance of sections, with the design fitting better in one section than in another. The wish to preserve a particularly unusual grain can also determine pattern placement. Work your pattern around, shifting as needed, to preserve as much of the distinctive grain as possible. The pattern can offer suggestions for placement, too. A bird coming in for a landing may be best placed off-center and near the top of the wood. Move the pattern around until you find the placement that you like best.

Pattern changes may be necessary when using natural-edged wood because secondary parts of the pattern sometimes overlap the wood edge. Often you can eliminate secondary parts without losing the

Modifying a Pattern To Fit Irregularly Shaped Wood

1. Check several placements of the pattern on the wood before deciding.
2. Eliminate or modify secondary parts of the pattern to fit or enhance the unusualness of the wood.
3. Cut and finish as desired.

Original Pattern

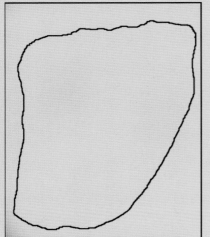

Irregular Wood Shape

New Pattern

Figure 20. Removing secondary parts so that a pattern fits on an irregularly shaped piece of wood creates a new pattern.

integrity and focal point of the design. **(See Figure 20.)**

Because slab and burl wood are harder to find than some other woods, I recommend buying them when you find them. Store them flat and wait for the right design to come along. If you have the perfect project but no slab or burl wood, create a similar look by cutting the edge of dimensioned wood. Cut as irregular and as rough as possible; then scorch or burn that same edge. **(See Figure 21.)**

USING OTHER MATERIALS

Consider trying materials other than wood. Although not all scroll saws have the capability to scroll materials other than wood, there are saws that will cut a wide variety of materials. Glass, metal, plastic, antler and even paper are a few of

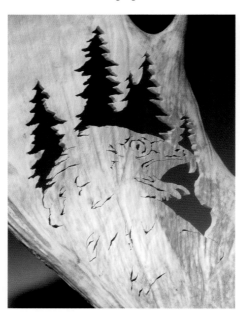

Figure 22. Antler is one material that can give a look not obtainable in wood.

Figure 21. If slab or burl wood isn't available to you, create a similar look by cutting the edge of the wood irregularly then burning or scoring the edge.

these alternate materials. **(See Figure 22.)** A project cut from one of these mediums can be very dramatic and infuse the project with a uniqueness not obtainable in wood.

Figure 23. The beads are a nice addition and add a bit of color and light to this project.

Figure 24. A log frame works very well with the textured leather and irregularly shaped wood in this project.

Figure 25. Pawprints cut into a frame can complement many wildlife projects.

Making Your Own Log Frame

1. Using your scroll saw, cut the logs lengthwise.
2. Measure for frame size and miter the ends.
3. Glue the frame together.
4. Glue the frame onto a plywood backing, if desired.

If you don't want to cut your project entirely from non-wood material, try integrating other materials into the wood project. Metal inlays nicely into wood; stone used as an overlay brings a little "Southwest" to the art. Set into a project, glass and plastic introduce light into a design. Be creative. Try something unique and unusual.

As you experiment with different techniques, remember that enhancing a design can be as simple as adding a few finishing touches. Stain or paint all or part of a project. Add beadwork, feathers, stones or antler. **(See Figure 23.)** When incorporated into a design, these additions can transform your project into a finished piece of art.

DISPLAYING A PROJECT

FRAMING

Sizes and styles of frames are endless, as are the ways they can be used. Because your choice can make or break a design, it is best to take the project with you when purchasing a frame. A deep shadow box with the design in the center is one use of a frame that creates a finished look. Gluing spacers between the project and the back will set off the design even more.

Making your own frame is another possibility. A log frame, for instance, is fairly easy to make. **(See Figure 24.)** Find four straight limbs. Using your scroll saw (thicker logs may require a bandsaw), slice the limbs lengthwise. Measure for frame size, miter the ends and glue the frame together. These limbs can also be glued to a plywood backing. A variation of this log frame is to forego the miters and overlap the corners, similar to building a log cabin.

Pre-formed molding is a good way to frame an odd-sized project. The cost of custom frames is very high. By using molding, you are able to make these frames at a fraction of the cost. Corner clamps are a big asset when making mitered frames.

To finish framing your project, try cutting a design that complements the project into the frame. **(See Figure 25.)** Like placement on a wood slab, don't always center the design. Combining different backdrops with different frames gives endless choices and unlimited potential.

Typically, framing involves using mat board and glass, but scrollers often discard these items. Don't be quite so fast to push these aside. Your next project may be the best time to use the mat and glass. A footprint, a feather or a touch of fret cut into the mat may well complete your project. An unusual use of glass is to put it behind the frame. Glue your project to the glass itself. This gives your design the illusion of floating within the frame.

If you don't want to make your own frame, custom frames are available to purchase. However, because custom-made frames are quite costly, keeping an eye open at garage sales and secondhand stores can be a big money saver.

OTHER METHODS

Although the traditional method of framing and hanging scroll saw designs makes a great presentation, try something else. Displaying your scroll saw project as an overlay for a glass window, as a freestanding piece, as functional art, as a window valance, as an inlay in cupboard doors or in floors, or as gingerbread will convey distinctiveness and individuality in your home. **(See Figure 26.)** Headboards of beds, backs of chairs, fireplace mantels, table edgings, belt buckles and key chains are all places where scrollwork can be found. The list goes on and on. Try integrating your pieces into your home—bear footprints inlaid into a wooden floor may create just the right atmosphere. One of the most unique displays of scroll saw work that I've ever seen was inside a log cabin. A slice was removed from a log in the wall, a design was cut into the slice, and the slice was glued back. The artwork became part of the log wall.

Stands are a display alternative

Figure 27. A natural stand can work well as the finishing touch for a project. This stand is part of a project cut in antler, shown on page 30.

for your art. Stone and driftwood, combined with a little work, make great stands. There are a few simple stands included in this book, but try some of your own ideas. **(See Figures 27 and 28.)**

CONCLUSION

Always keep in mind that the original designs or the original intentions for the designs are not set in stone. Just because an original pattern was not drawn or intended to be scrolled or displayed in a certain manner does not prevent you from making minor changes, scrolling it differently, or displaying the final piece in another way.

When you take artistic risks and experiment with changing a pattern, you gain one of two results: 1) the development of your artistic ability or 2) "designer firewood." I must admit that I've had my share of designer firewood, but the more pattern changes I make, the less

this happens. So I encourage you to stretch your creativity, to extend your imagination and to test your limits. Don't be afraid to try anything, even if you are not always successful. Each failure and each success will help you create your own personal artistic style.

Figure 26. This inlaid blanket chest by Dan Riepe is an example of one way to add individuality to your home.

Figure 28. This simple stand creates a clean finish.

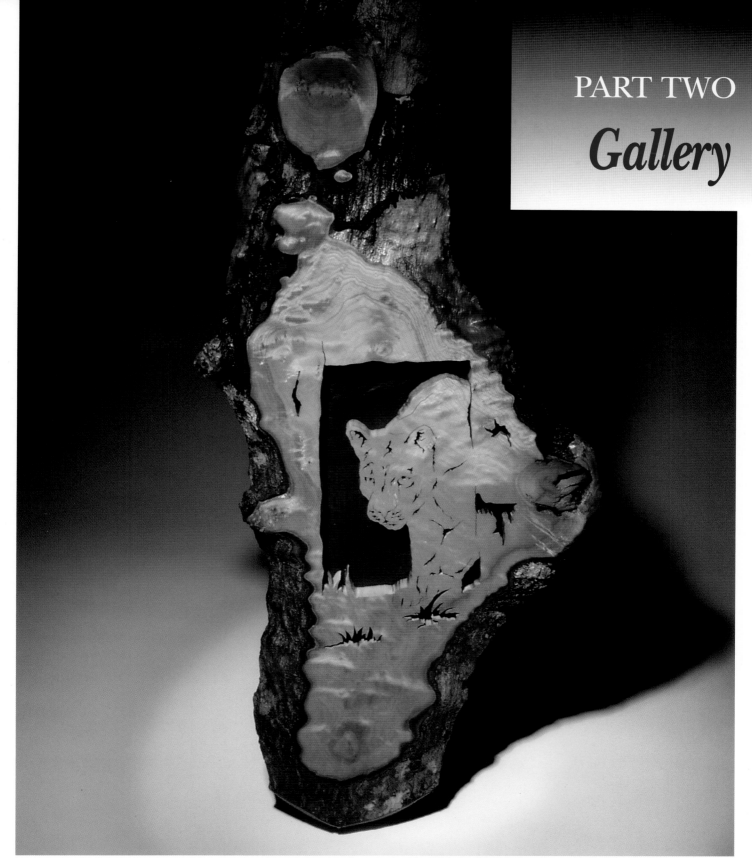

COUGAR

Naturally shaped wood with bark attached can be a big asset to wildlife.
The pattern for this project is found on page 66.

COUGAR

The correct frame can be the finishing touch to a project. In this project, the
white background offsets the dark wood. The pattern for this project is found
on page 67.

KESTREL FALCON

Cut from a throwaway piece of wood. The pattern for this project is found on
page 55.

TIGER

Because of the grain in this wood, the tiger seems to be a part of the wood
instead of being cut from it. The pattern for this project is found on page 79.

GOLDEN EAGLE

A simple stand with the addition of beads contributes both color and light to
this piece. The pattern for this project is found on pages 38 and 39.

JAGUAR

A man-made edge can be very effective and can give the look of slab wood.
The dark backdrop contributes to the contrasts found in a jaguar's fur.
The pattern for this project is found on pages 80 and 81.

GRIZZLY BEAR

Natural burl complements wildlife. The pattern for this project is found on
page 104.

CHEETAH

A design added to a purchased frame is another option to explore. The
pattern for this project is found on page 85.

RED-SHOULDERED HAWK

Cleanup and some paint turned this garage sale frame into the finishing touch
for this project. The pattern for this project is found on page 49.

COUGAR AND CUB

The addition of the leaves and framing as an overlay added interest and depth
to this design. The patterns for this project are found on pages 68 and 69.

EAGLE

Actual feathers were used to "frame" this wooden feather. The pattern for this
project is found on page 57.

GRIZZLY BEAR

Cut from Corian, this grizzly bear is easily turned into a piece of jewelry. The
pattern for this project is found on page 104.

GRIZZLY BEAR

The cinnamon color of this wood was the perfect choice for a grizzly bear. Notice
the very simple stand. The patterns for this project are found on page 102.

GRIZZLY BEAR

Designs cut into portions of firewood can make use of even the smallest scrap.
The pattern for this project is found on page 103.

BOBCAT

Experiment with different ways of finishing and framing. The pattern for this
project is found on page 76.

RED-TAILED HAWK

Cut from moose antler, this piece rests beautifully upon a stand made from
natural tree root. The pattern for this project is found on page 48.

PART THREE

Patterns
North American
Birds of Prey

The warmth of the sun upon his back,
He rides the currents of the sky.
With a graceful wave of his wings,
He dances with the clouds.
—*Carmin*

The bald eagle's head and tail turn completely white by the age of five.

© Marilyn Carmin

© Marilyn Carmin

A

B

© Marilyn Carmin

A 7" x 9 ¹/₂" American flag fits
beautifully behind this design.

© Marilyn Carmin

© Marilyn Carmin

B

A

© Marilyn Carmin

The golden eagle's range covers the whole Northern Hemisphere and may be the widest range of any eagle on earth.

© Marilyn Carmin

A

B

© Marilyn Carmin

© Marilyn Carmin

© Marilyn Carmin

Artistic Wildlife Projects for the Scroll Saw

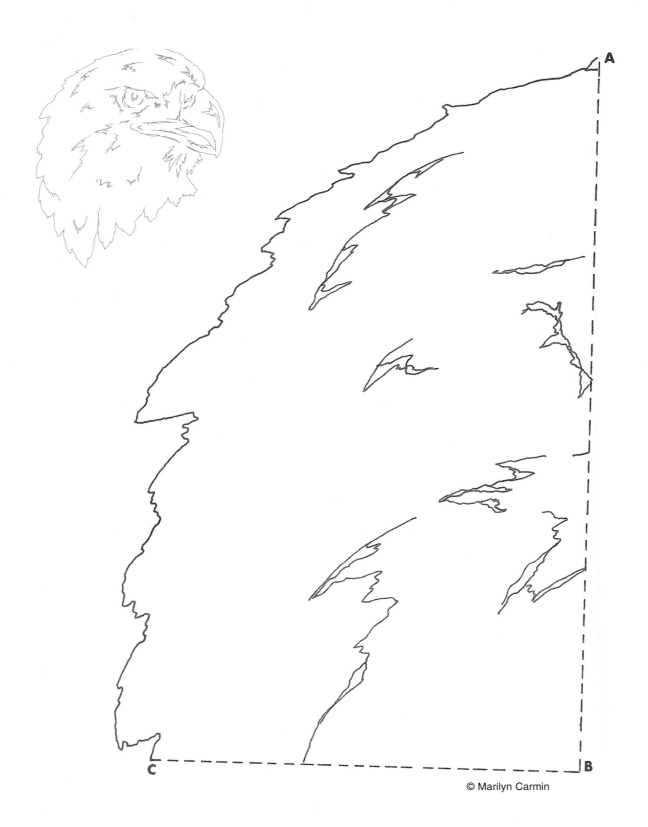

© Marilyn Carmin

© Marilyn Carmin

There are only two eagles that call
North America home: the golden
eagle and the bald eagle.

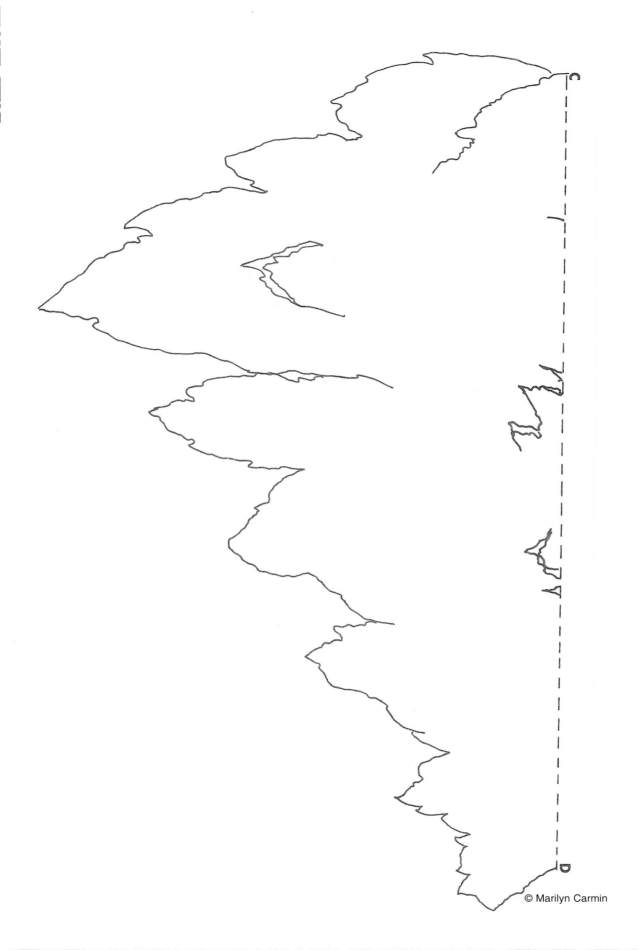

© Marilyn Carmin

© Marilyn Carmin

A © Marilyn Carmin

B

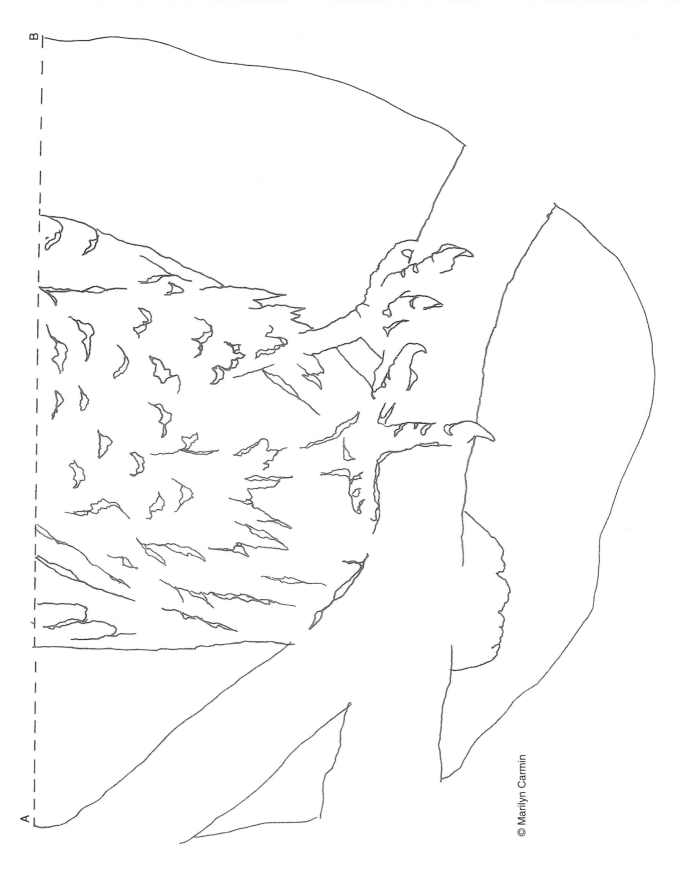

B

A

© Marilyn Carmin

© Marilyn Carmin

The red-shouldered hawk gets its name from the rich reddish-brown patch on each shoulder.

© Marilyn Carmin

© Marilyn Carmin

© Marilyn Carmin

© Marilyn Carmin

Owls are the silent hunters of the sky, their feathers' shapes making them virtually noiseless.

© Marilyn Carmin

© Marilyn Carmin

The kestrel is the smallest and most common of the falcons.

Artistic Wildlife Projects for the Scroll Saw

© Marilyn Carmin

Vultures have a very distinctive flight.
Their wings are held in a shallow V,
and they rock from side to side, only
rarely flapping their wings.

© Marilyn Carmin

© Marilyn Carmin

© Marilyn Carmin

A

B

© Marilyn Carmin

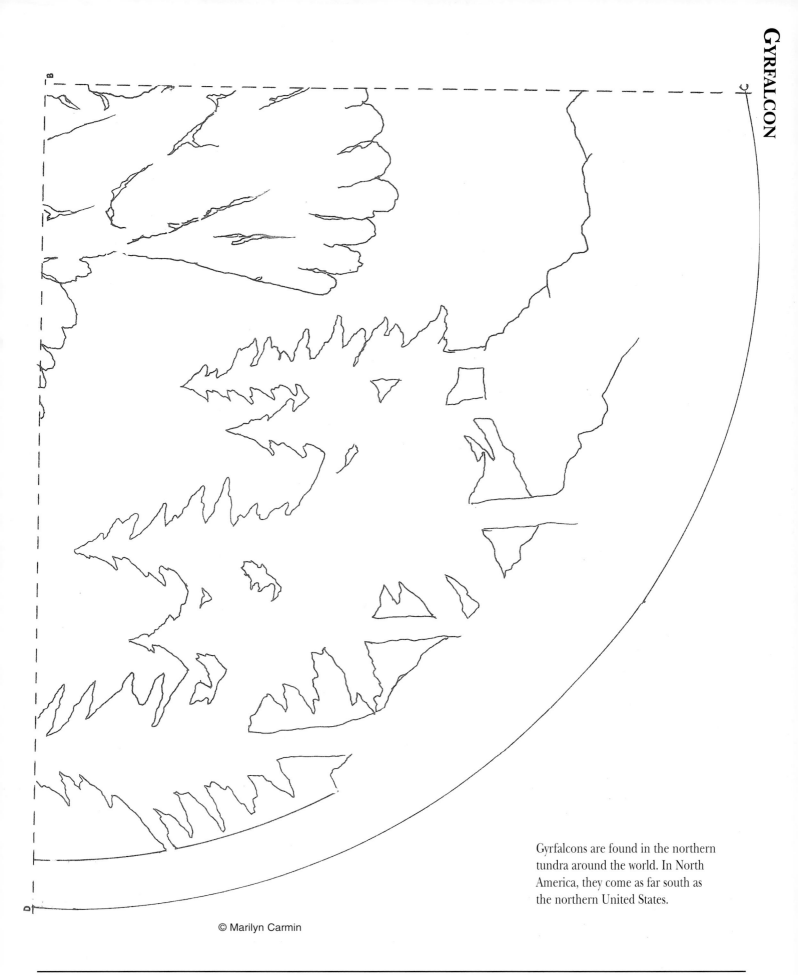

B

C

D

Gyrfalcons are found in the northern tundra around the world. In North America, they come as far south as the northern United States.

© Marilyn Carmin

A

E

B

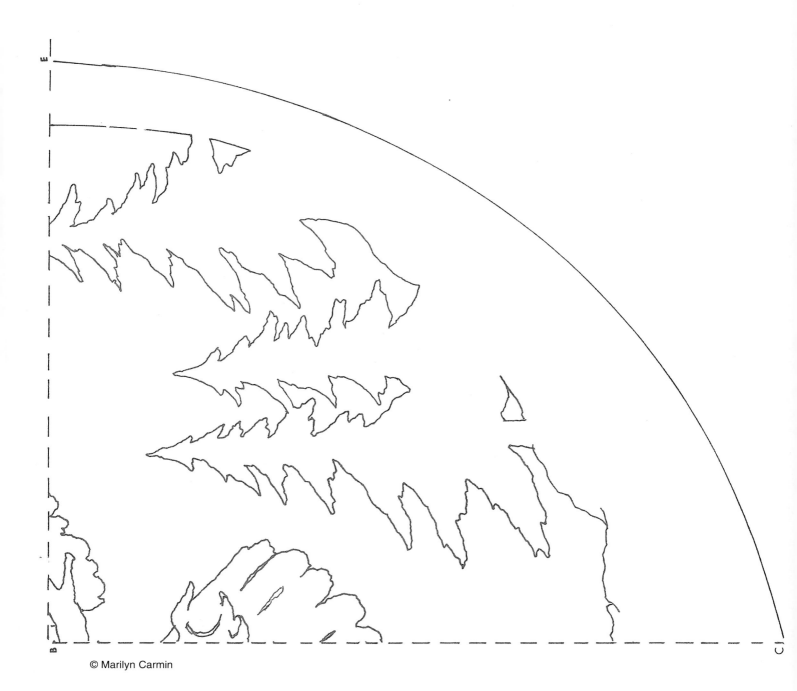

E

B

C

© Marilyn Carmin

© Marilyn Carmin

North American Cats

A hint of a presence, the feeling he's close
The movement of shadow, a flick of a tail
And he silently moves by.
—*Carmin*

At over 200 pounds and over nine feet long, the cougar is North America's big cat. Females are about one-third smaller than the males.

© Marilyn Carmin

© Marilyn Carmin

Mountain lions are also known as pumas, cougars,
shadow cats, cats'o'mount and panthers.

© Marilyn Carmin

© Marilyn Carmin

© Marilyn Carmin

B

E

C

© Marilyn Carmin

© Marilyn Carmin

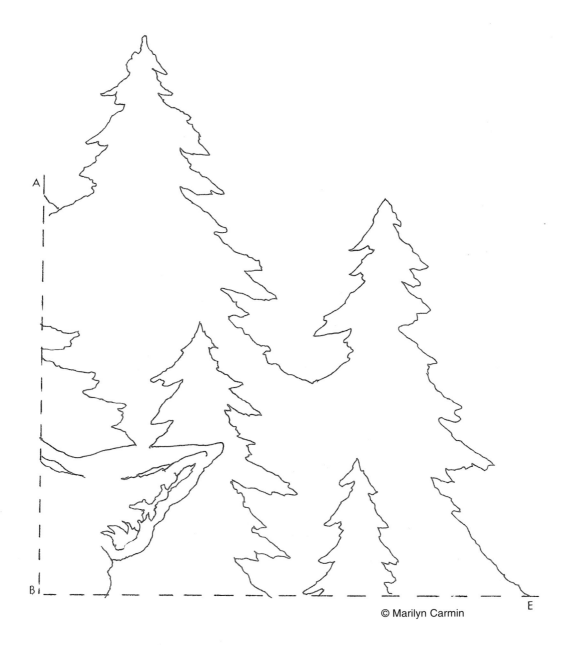

A

B

E

© Marilyn Carmin

© Marilyn Carmin

© Marilyn Carmin

© Marilyn Carmin

A mature male bobcat weighs around 15 to 25 pounds, stands 22 inches at the shoulder, and measures about 4 feet in length. Females are slightly smaller.

Around two inches long, the ear tufts
of a lynx are more prominent than
those of a bobcat.

© Marilyn Carmin

© Marilyn Carmin

© Marilyn Carmin

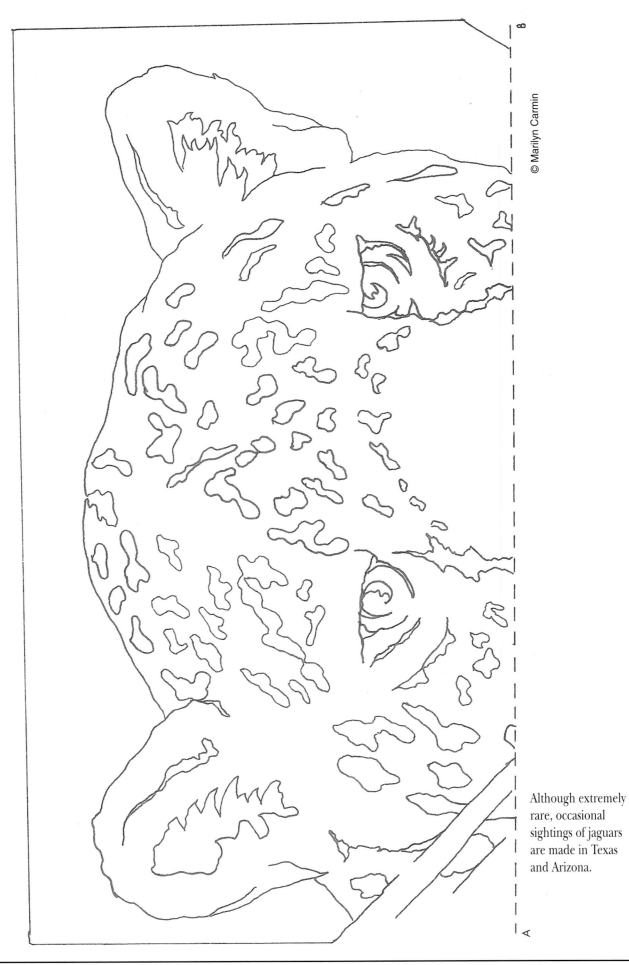

© Marilyn Carmin

B

Although extremely
rare, occasional
sightings of jaguars
are made in Texas
and Arizona.

A

© Marilyn Carmin

A

B

© Marilyn Carmin

A

B

© Marilyn Carmin

C

D

© Marilyn Carmin

© Marilyn Carmin

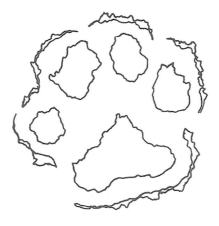

Lynx

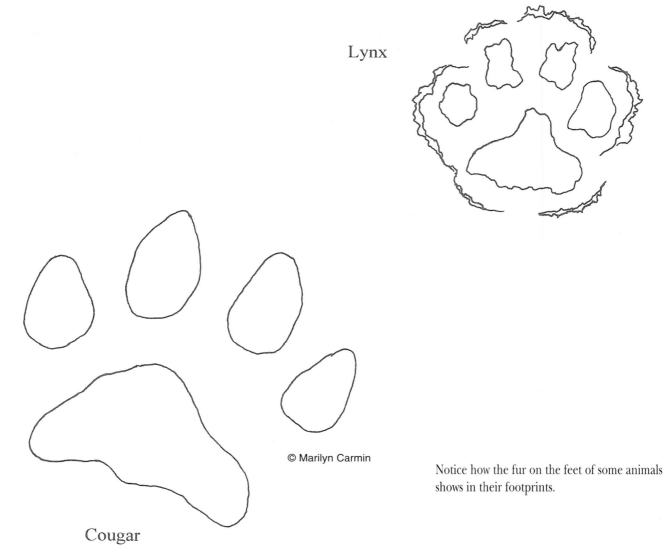

© Marilyn Carmin

Notice how the fur on the feet of some animals shows in their footprints.

Cougar

North American Canines

The intenseness of his stare
Reaches right to the soul
The yellow eyes locked and unwavering.

His body, tight and controlled
As he creeps toward his goal
His focus remains unchanging.

Then with the blink of his eye,
The tension is gone
Interest is lost, it's not worthy.

Resting in the shadows,
The hunter remains
Watching, searching and patiently waiting.

—*Carmin*

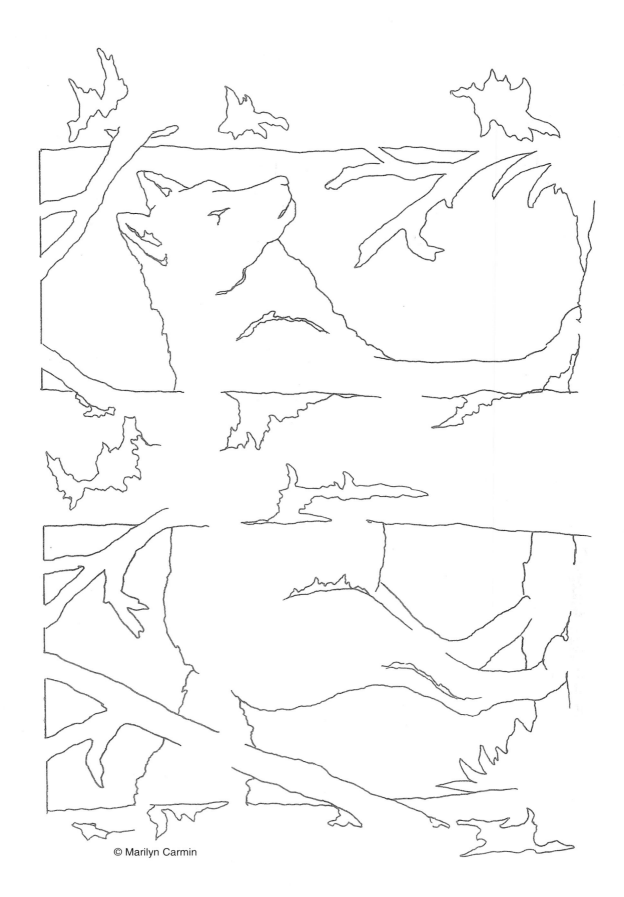

© Marilyn Carmin

© Marilyn Carmin

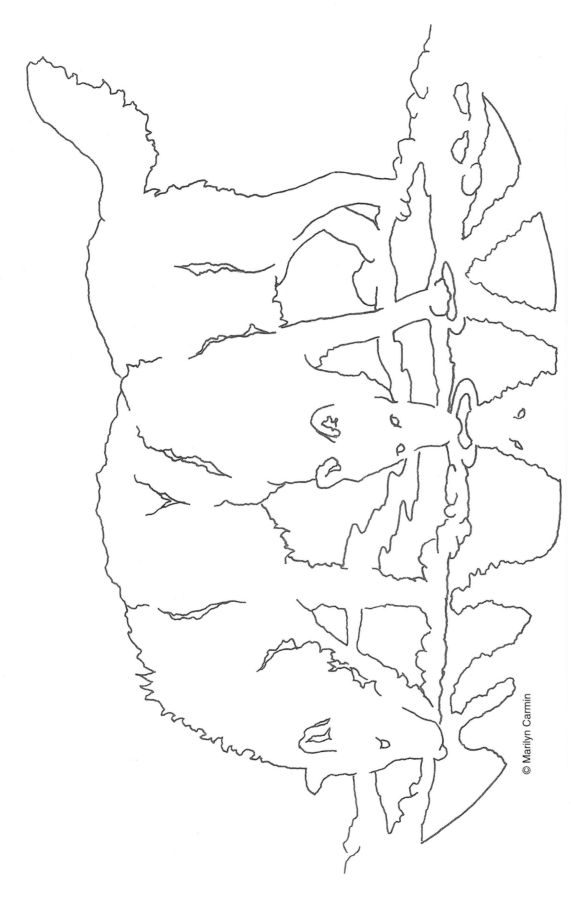

© Marilyn Carmin

© Marilyn Carmin

The gray wolf plays a very important role in maintaining the balance of nature, even though the range where it still roams is very limited.

© Marilyn Carmin

© Marilyn Carmin

© Marilyn Carmin

© Marilyn Carmin

© Marilyn Carmin

© Marilyn Carmin

The coyote is one of North America's most adaptable wild animals. The coyote's range covers most of Canada and the United States. Coyotes live quite success-fully near humans.

© Marilyn Carmin

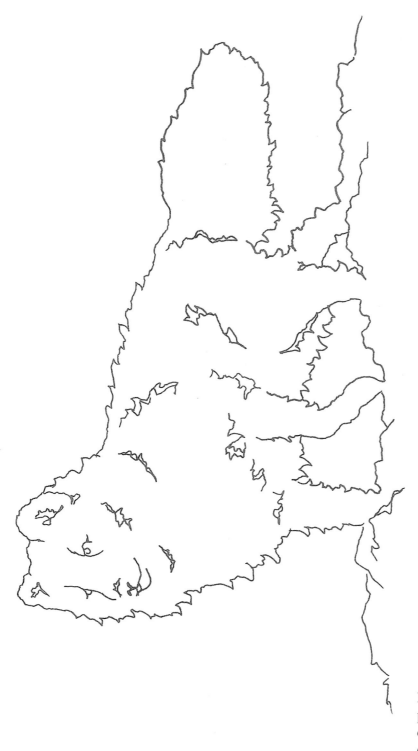

© Marilyn Carmin

During the winter, arctic foxes will "adopt" polar bears, following them around and eating scraps left behind. However, they do need to watch that they do not become the bear's next meal.

Wolf

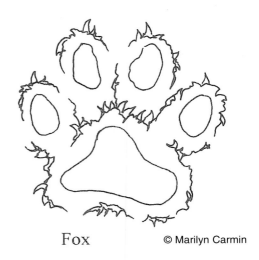

Fox

© Marilyn Carmin

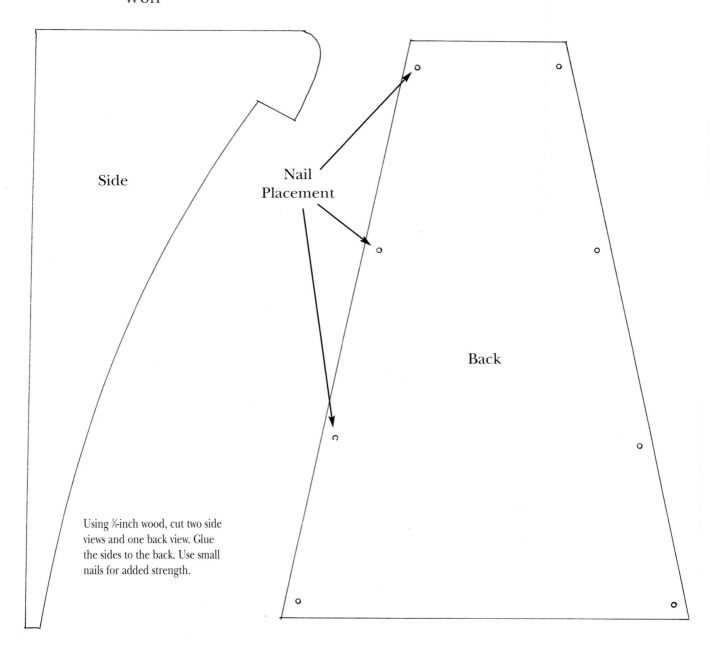

Side

Nail
Placement

Back

Using ¾-inch wood, cut two side
views and one back view. Glue
the sides to the back. Use small
nails for added strength.

North American Bears

With no concept of the power of sound,
I hear the grizzly's growl.

Fingers of fear wrap around me.
My heart beats double time as the sound imbeds
itself in every part of my being.

A deep, low rumble, growing, building, reaching,
gripping, consuming!
This indescribable, awesome sound!

The grizzly's angry growl.
—*Carmin*

Although they are the same classification, "brown bears" usually refers to bears found in the coastal regions, and "grizzlies" are those found inland.

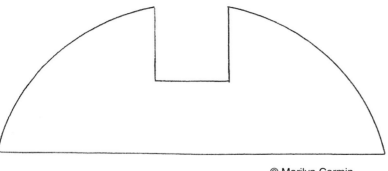

© Marilyn Carmin

This stand is a very simple one. Cut two pieces from ¾-inch or thicker wood. The inside groove needs to be the width of the project to be displayed.

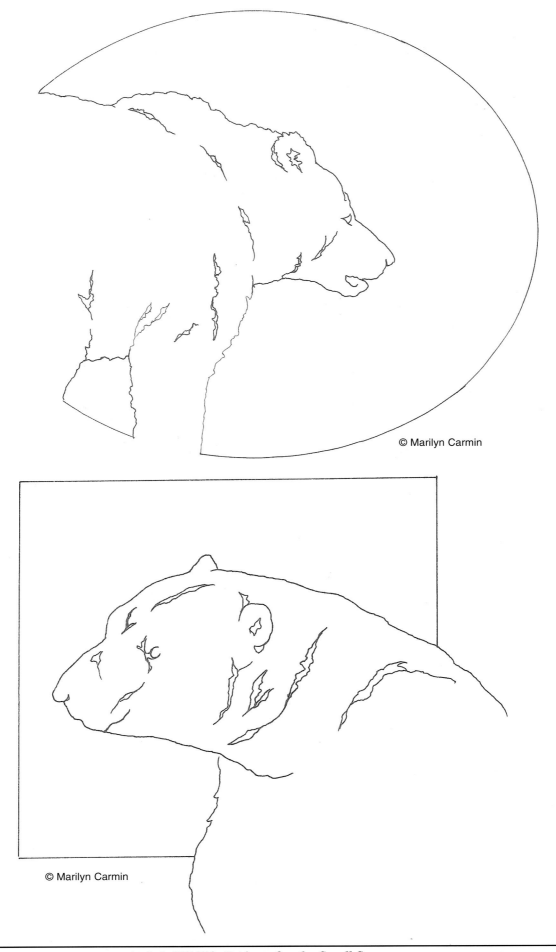

© Marilyn Carmin

© Marilyn Carmin

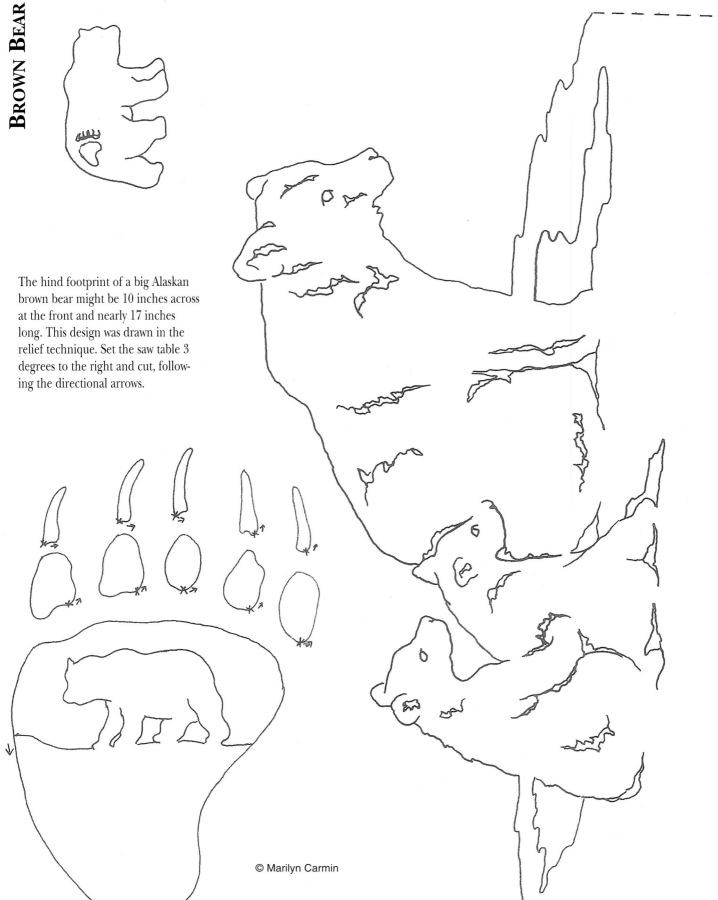

The hind footprint of a big Alaskan brown bear might be 10 inches across at the front and nearly 17 inches long. This design was drawn in the relief technique. Set the saw table 3 degrees to the right and cut, following the directional arrows.

© Marilyn Carmin

© Marilyn Carmin

© Marilyn Carmin

© Marilyn Carmin

Black bear cubs weigh approximately five pounds when leaving the den for the first time. By mid-summer they can weigh 30 pounds.

© Marilyn Carmin

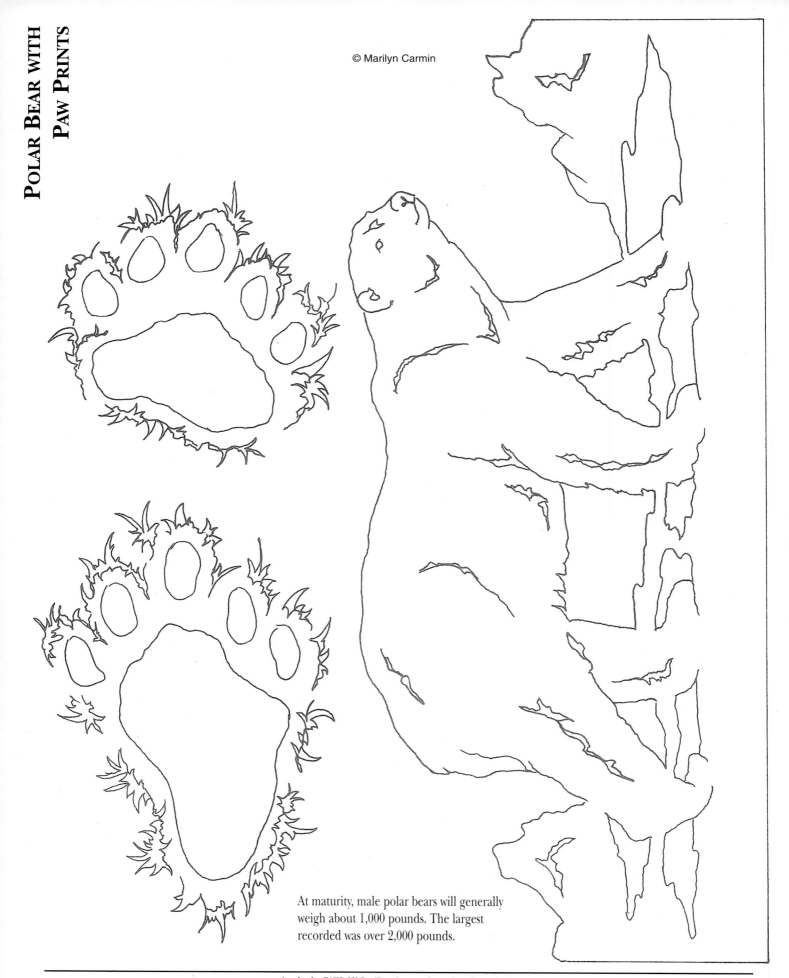

At maturity, male polar bears will generally weigh about 1,000 pounds. The largest recorded was over 2,000 pounds.

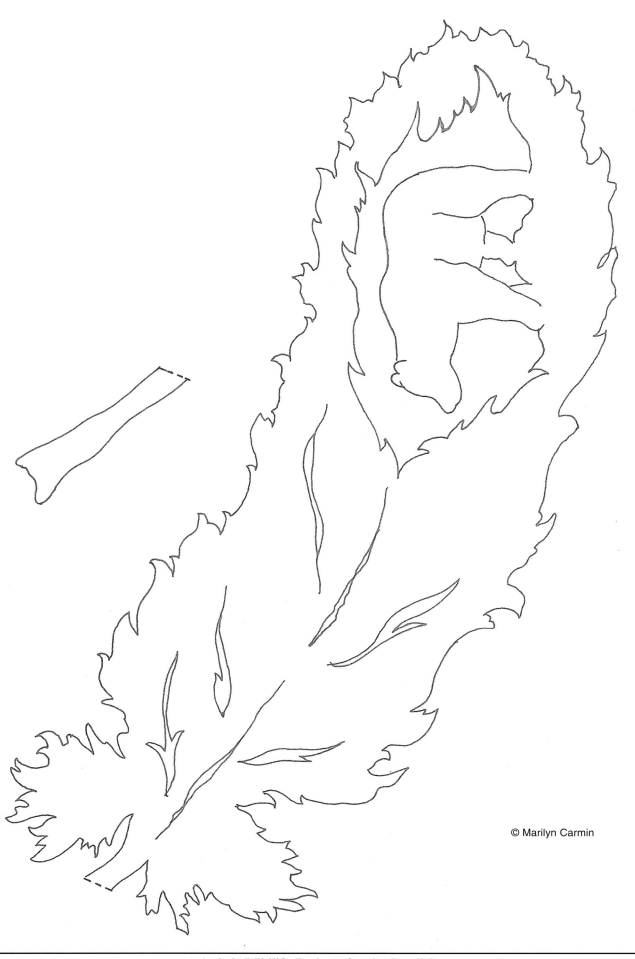

© Marilyn Carmin

© Marilyn Carmin

A

B

A

B

© Marilyn Carmin

© Marilyn Carmin

© Marilyn Carmin

More Great Project Books from Fox Chapel Publishing

- **Scroll Saw Relief Projects by Marilyn Carmin:** Turn your favorite fretwork pattern info something special with the techniques found in this book. Features tips and techniques for scroll saw relief and relief/fret combinations. ISBN: 1-56523-107-4, 112 pages, soft cover, $14.95.

- **North American Wildlife Patterns for the Scroll Saw by Lora S. Irish:** Bring North American animals to life with the exciting scroll saw patterns found in this book. Choose from more than 50 ready-to-cut patterns that include everything from squirrels, raccoons and rabbits to moose, cougars and rams. Each pattern is drawn with crisp, easy-to-follow lines. ISBN: 1-56523-165-1, 72 pages, soft cover, $12.95.

- **DEER: Ultimate Artist's Reference Guide by Doug Lindstrand:** A vast collection of artwork and reference material for deer. Inside you will find over 150 full-color photographs for deer at various ages and in various seasons, over 100 sketches, anatomical measurements, first hand accounts of deer in motion, and more. All North American species included! ISBN: 1-56523-195-3, 112 pages, soft cover, $19.95.

- **Great Book of Dragon Patterns 2nd Edition by Lora S. Irish:** A guide for creating your own fantastic renderings of man's favorite foe-the dragon! History, anatomy and patterns for all types of dragons from worms through Arthurian. The revised version of this popular title now includes over 100 dragon patterns plus information on the oriental dragon. ISBN: 1-565623-231-3, 188 pages, soft cover, $19.95.

- **Great Book of Fairy Patterns by Lora S. Irish:** Create your own fairy art in a variety of mediums including painting, tattooing, woodworking, illustrations, and more. Over 70 patterns are included along with tips, techniques, anatomy, gallery and more. ISBN: 1-56523-225-9, 192 pages, soft cover, $19.95

- **BEAR: Ultimate Artist's Reference Guide by Doug Lindstrand:** A must-have reference for anyone interested bear. Inside you will find over 150 stunning full-color photographs for bear in their natural habitat. You'll also find over 100 sketches providing up-close detail for paws, mouth and other parts. Black, Grizzly and Polar Bear all included. ISBN: 1-56523-214-3, 112 pages, soft cover, $19.95.

- **World Wildlife Patterns for the Scroll Saw by Lora S. Irish:** by Lora S. Irish: More than 50 superbly rendered patterns of wild animals from all over the globe including panda bears, kangaroos, elephants, lions, gorillas, monkeys and much more! ISBN: 1-56523-167-8, 72 pages, soft cover, $12.95.

- **Marine Life Patterns for the Scroll Saw by Dale Terrian:** Scroll all varieties of underwater creatures: dolphins, seahorses, whales, trout, sailfish, salmon and more. Includes over 50 patterns and great painting/finishing techniques. ISBN: 1-56523-167-8, 72 pages, soft cover, $12.95.

- **Drawing Mammals 3rd Edition by Doug Lindstrand:** Color photographs, sketches, and notes on twenty of North America's favorite large animals. Includes bears, coyotes, wolves, mountain lions, pronghorns, bison, mountain goats, sheep, caribou, deer, elk, and moose. Recently revised with 40 new color photographs! ISBN: 1-56523-206-2, 212 pages, soft cover, $25.00

- **Drawing America's Wildlife 2nd Edition by Doug Lindstrand:** Animals, birds, and fish come to life in this fully revised portfolio that includes field sketches, drawings of footprints, and four-color photographs of more than 60 species of North American animals taken in their natural habitats. A great reference for carvers! ISBN: 1-56523-203-8, 216 pages, soft cover, $25.00.

CHECK WITH YOUR LOCAL WOODWORKING STORE OR BOOK RETAILER
Or call 800-457-9112 • Visit www.foxchapelpublishing.com